© Copyright 2016

Written by Sally A Jones and Amanda C Jones
Illustrations by Annalisa Jones

Published by GUINEA PIG EDUCATION

2 Cobs Way,
New Haw,
Addlestone,
Surrey,
KT15 3AF.
www.guineapigeducation.co.uk

NO part of this publication may be reproduced, stored or copied for commercial purposes and profit without the prior written permission of the publishers.

ISBN: 9781910824023

Dear kids,

If you work through this book, you will learn to write letters. You will also learn how to write lots of facts about yourself and to write about how you feel about the things you do.

Dear adults,

A lively collection of ideas to improve your child's writing. He or she will learn to set out a letter and to write using facts and opinions.

This book is a starting point to get your child to enjoy writing. All the ideas have been trialled in tutorial classes, with children of 6-9 years. For younger children, we advise that the adult works through the book with the child. Older children, who are fluent readers, will have fun completing the book themselves.

If we saturate our children with good ideas and vocabulary in the early years, we can assist them in their writing and build on the work they do at school.

Find a notebook.

Write down some facts.

On each page, make a heading:

1. 'About Me'

2. 'My School'

3. 'My Friends'

4. 'My Birthday'

5. 'Where I Live'

6. 'My Garden'

7. 'My Pets'

Copy and complete the sentences with information that is true.

What is a FACT?

It is a piece of information that is true.

You have a new friend called Carmen who lives in South Africa. Carmen writes you a letter.

Pretoria,
South Africa.

24th September.

Dear ....,

My name is Carmen and I live in South Africa. I am an only child. There are three people in my family. They are my mum, my dad and me.

I have brown eyes and black, curly hair. I like to wear my jeans and a t-shirt.

My school is in Pretoria. I go to school on the bus and we learn to read, write and do maths.

It is hot and sunny in South Africa, so I ride my bike every day when I get home from school.

My house is big and it has a wall all the way round. It has a gate with a security system to let you in or out. I have four dogs.

My garden is large too and it has mango and pepper trees growing in it. Weaver birds nest in the trees.

Please write and tell me about your life in England.

Love from,

Carmen

xx

What can I tell you about me?

1. My name is ....
   ....

2. I live in ....

3. I have .... brothers and sisters.

4. There are .... people in my family.

5. They are my .... and ....

6. I have .... eyes.

7. I have .... hair.

8. I am wearing a .... t-shirt and a ....trousers/skirt.

Draw a picture of yourself.

                                              My Address,
                                              ....,
                                              ....
                                              ....

                                              Date.

Dear Carmen,

      I am pleased that you are going to be my friend. I will write to you every month.

My name is .... I live in .... I have .... brothers and sisters. There are .... people in my family.

I have .... eyes and .... hair. My favourite clothes are ....
....

I hope that you are well.

                Love

              ....

                xx

REMEMBER...

What can I tell you about my school?

Draw a picture of your school.

1. I go to .... school.

2. I go there by ....

3. I am in year ....

4. My teacher is called ....

5. In my classroom there is a ....
   and ....

6. My favourite school lunch is ....
   ....

My School Day

On Monday I do ....

On Tuesday I do ....

On Wednesday I do ....

On Thursday I do ....

On Friday I do ....

The one I like best is ....

....

....

My favourite subject...

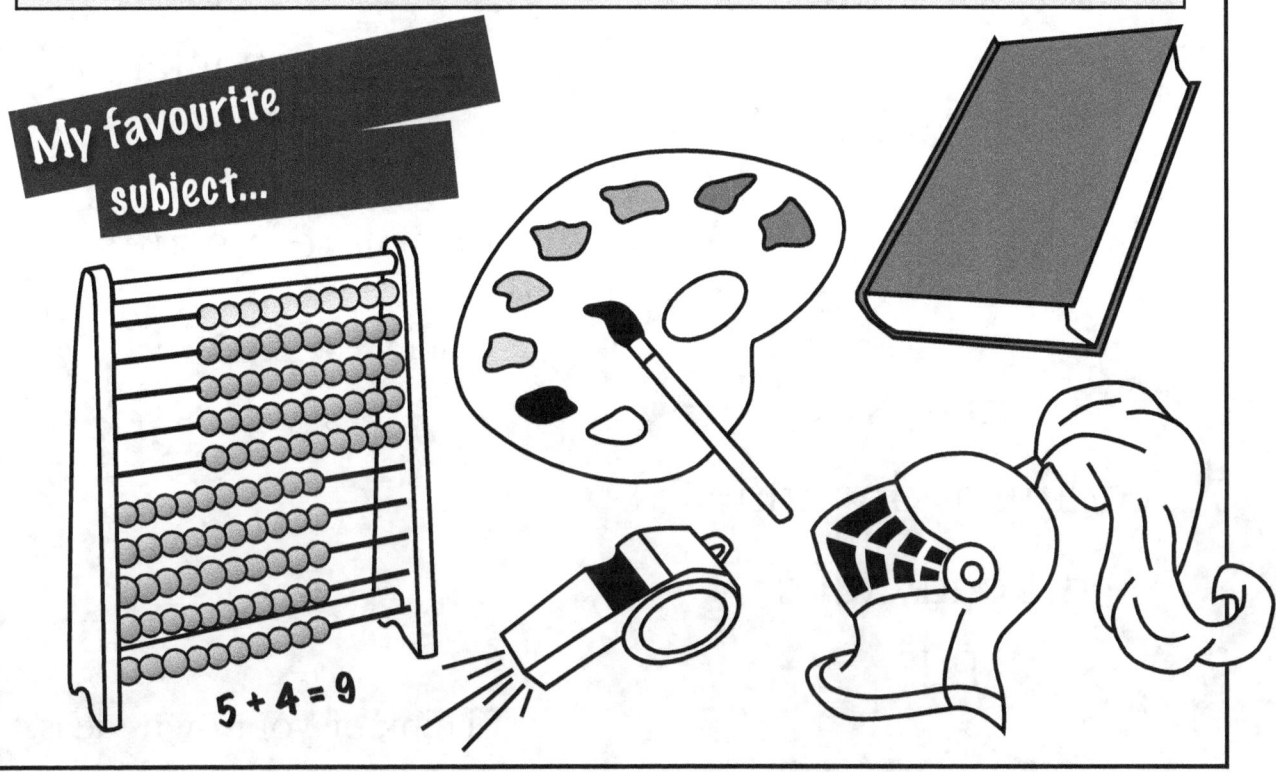

5 + 4 = 9

Some ideas:

Mrs ...
Mr ...

train
car
bus

computer
interactive white board
reading books
work on the walls

a packed lunch
school dinner

healthy snacks
sandwiches
chocolate biscuits
apples, raisins

maths
reading and writing
art and craft
P.E

Think of your own ideas.

My Address,

..................,

....

Date.

Dear Carmen,

Thank you for the letter you sent me telling me about your school. It was very interesting.

I go to .... school and I am in year .... The teacher is called .... and she is very kind.

In my classroom there is an .... and .... My favourite lesson is .... because we do ....

I hope you have a good week at school.

Love

....

xx

What can I tell you about my friends?

Maggie has .... eyes and .... hair.

Tom has .... eyes and .... hair.

Pete has .... eyes and .... hair.

My Best Friend

My best friend is ....
....

He/she is ....
.... old.

He/she lives at ....
....

There are .... people in his/her family.

He/she has .... eyes and .... hair.

He/she wears ....
....

Draw a picture of your best friend.

Some ideas:

bright blue
brown
hazel

blonde
curly
short black
long

trousers
jeans   socks
skirt   shoes
t-shirt a hat
jumper dress

My Address,

..................,

....

Date.

Dear Carmen,

Thank you for your letter. I enjoyed reading about your friends in Pretoria. One day I would like to come and meet them.

I have a best friend too and she is called .... She is the same age as me, so she is .... She lives at ....

My friend is very bossy and chooses what games we play. Her eyes are .... and her hair is .... Her favourite clothes are ....

I will think of you playing with your friends.

Love

....

What can I tell you about my birthday?

I was ....
.... years old.

I had a ....
.... party.

It was at ....

The friends who came to my party were:

....

....

At the party we ....

After this we ....
and ....

The presents I had were ....
....

I enjoyed it because ....
....

Some ideas:

princess party
swimming party
bouncy castle party
bowling party
fancy dress party

ate cake
played party games
blew out candles
face painting
danced to music

My Address,

..................,

....

Date.

Dear Carmen,

Thank you for your letter. I am glad that you are enjoying riding your new bike in the sun. It is winter in England and icy cold.

It was my birthday on .... I had a party at .... and I invited .... of my friends. At the party we .... and then we ....

When I got home I opened my presents and I had a .... It was fun.

Have fun riding your bike.

Love

....

What can I tell you about where I live?

Draw a picture of your house.

My address is ....

It is in the ....

My house is ....

My house has ....

My street is ....

In my street you see ....

Some ideas:

- the town
- the country

- quiet
- noisy
- busy

- a big house
- a small house
- a bungalow
- a flat
- a huge house

- red flowers
- trees

- a post box
- a parked car

What can I tell you about my garden?

My garden is ....

....

In my garden there is ......

....

Flowers that grow in my garden are ....

This wild life visits my garden: ....

....

When I am in my garden I like to ....
and ....

I love my garden because ....

....

Draw a picture of your garden

Some ideas:

- large
- small
- tiny

- patio
- lawn
- shed

- have a barbeque
- play in my paddling pool
- put up my tent
- feed the birds
- build a snow man

- roses
- geraniums
- daffodil

- black bird
- squirrel
- hedgehog
- fox

My Address,

...................,

....

Date.

Dear Carmen,

　　　　Thank you for your letter. It must be fun to live in a big, walled house with a gate. Do your dogs guard your house?

I wish I had a big garden to play in with mango and pepper trees growing in it. I have never seen a weaver bird because we do not have them in England.

My house is .... in a very .... street. It has a .... with a .... There is also a ....

My garden is .... It has a .... There are many plants like ....

There is also a lot of wildlife that visits my garden: hedgehogs, foxes, blackbirds, ... In summer, in my garden, I enjoy .... In winter, I like to ....

I would love to see a picture of your dogs.

　　　　　　　Love
　　　　　　..................

Now let's write some OPINIONS

An opinion is a piece of information that may not be true.

They are how people feel about things.

Let me tell you about the pets I have...

My pet is a ....

My pet is called ....

It is .... years old.

It is .... colour.

It has ....

My Pet

I love him/her because ....

....

My friend/nana/grandad has a ....

....

Some ideas:

Use some <u>DESCRIBING</u> WORDS to make your writing more interesting.

bright eyes   soft fur

black spots   pointy ears

a wet nose   long whiskers

a fluffy tail   sharp claws

good
naughty
mischievous

pointy
soft   sharp
floppy   black
waggly   long

Describing words are adjectives.

                                                My Address,
                                                ....,
                                                 ....
                                                 Date.

Dear Carmen,

      Thank you for your letter. I like your dogs. Do they bark a lot? I hope they don't scare the weaver birds who are nesting in your garden, so the eggs do not hatch.

I have a pet .... He is ....
His colours are .... He has ....
....

I love him very much because ....
....
....

I look forward to hearing from you.
                    Love

                 ....

Let me tell you about my favourite toy...

FACT

I have these toys: ....

....

....

I have a set of: ....

....

My favourite toy

OPINION

My favourite toy is ....

I like it because ....

....

When I play with it I feel ....

....

When I was little my favourite toy was ....

....

Some ideas:

> I love my brio because I can build a big railway track.

> I enjoy playing with my lego because I can build a big tower.

> My teddy is my favourite toy because I take him to bed and cuddle him at night.

Let me tell you about my favourite food...

My favourite dinner is ....
....

Draw your favourite food:

It looks like this.

It tastes ....

It smells ....

It feels .... in your mouth.

I can hear .... as I chew it.

Foods I like:	Foods I do not like:
I like pasta carbonara because it is creamy, delicious and tasty. Pasta is healthy.	I do not like .... because ....
....	....
....	....

These things I collect:

- Stamps
- Postcards
- Brio
- Lego
- Shells
- ....
- ....
- ....

Add to this list.

I like to collect .... because ....
....
....

These are some places I have visited:

- The Natural History Museum
- The Science Museum
- The British Museum
- Theme Parks
- Bird Parks
- Farm Parks
- Seaside

I liked it there because ....
....
....
....

I did not like it there because ....
....
....
....

These are some of the places I have visited:

I went to .... with my .... and ....

We went there by ....

The weather was ....

When we got there, we saw ....
and ....

After this, we ....

For our lunch, we had .... in
....

My favourite part was ....
....
....

My Address,

...................,

....

Date.

Dear Carmen,

    Thank you for your letter. I loved hearing about your visit to the game reserve. It must have been very exciting to see the giraffes strolling by and get close to a big black leopard. Did you hear the lions roaring?

I went to London Zoo with my family on the tube. The weather was rainy. When we got there, we saw a tiger. He was sitting in his enclosure, behind the glass. I wanted to cuddle him because he did not look scary at all. After this, we saw the monkeys and bears.

My favourite part was penguin feeding time. They looked so cute waddling about as they gobbled up their fish. I bought a furry snake from the souvenir shop.

Love,

....

Now write your own letter with your own information.

Dear ....

I am at .... The

weather is ....

I have played in the sand and swam in the sea. The food is delicious.

Love,

....

What can I tell you about my holiday?

I went to .... for .... weeks, with my ....

We went there by .... and we stayed in a ....

The weather was ....

When we got there I visited ....
....

After this, I went on ....
....

I explored ....
....

I saw ....

I played with .... I made
these new friends ....

I ate these new foods ....

I enjoyed my holiday because ....
....

I did not enjoy ....
....

A drawing of my holiday.

My Address,

..................,

....

Date.

Dear Carmen,

        Thank you for your postcard from Cape Town. The mountains look very beautiful. Did you go in the cable car up to the top of Table Mountain? You must have seen some wonderful views.

In the summer holiday, I went on holiday with my family to the South of France. We drove in the car all night. I thought that it took a long time to get there, because we had to keep stopping to feed my dog that was travelling in the back.

When we got there, it was hot and sunny every day. I went swimming in the turquoise sea with my inflatable. I built sand castles in the golden sand. I collected some amazing shells.

What I enjoyed most was that my dog was there. He loved running along the sand and over the rocks. He liked the big garden near our apartment, because he could run down to the river and paddle his paws in the water. It was fun taking him to the vet, but the vet spoke to us in French and I knew my dad didn't understand a word.

Please write and tell me more about your holiday.

Love,

....

Now write your own letter with your own information.

Here are some more ideas for your own booklet.

- MY HOLIDAY
- MY FIRST VISIT TO THE ICE RINK.
- MY VISIT TO THE FUN FAIR.
- MY TRIP TO THE SEASIDE.
- MY TRIP TO THE RIVER.
- MY VISIT TO THE SUMMER FAIR.
- MY VISIT TO THE MUSEUM.
- MY TRIP TO SANTA'S GROTTO.

These are some questions to help you:

1. Where did you go?

   ....

   ....

2. Who did you go with?

   ....

3. What was the weather like?

   ....

4. How did you get there?

   ....

5. What did you do when you got there?

   ....

   ....

   ....

6. What did you do after that?

   ....
   ....
   ....
   ....

7. What did you like best about your visit?

   ....
   ....
   ....
   ....
   ....

Draw a picture

Isabella's Diary

My trip to West Farm.

In the school holiday, we went to West Farm. I went with my grandma and grandad and my auntie. We drove there in the car and it took about 20 minutes.

When I arrived at the farm, we walked through a big barn. There were lots of sit and ride toys for younger children. My little brother enjoyed riding on them.

After this, we saw lots of cuddly rabbits and guinea pigs, in their hutches. Some of them had babies. There were some horses, donkeys and alpacas in pens too.

The most exciting part of my visit was the pig race. We had to stand round a field. We cheered as the pigs ran fast up one side of the field and across the top until they reached the food. Pinky was the winner.

The activity I liked best was the playground. It was a huge adventure playground with an assault course. There were lots of things to climb and balance on.

My trip to Windsor

In the summer holiday, I went to Windsor with my mum and dad. We went in the car and the weather was hot and sunny.

When we had parked the car, we walked up the High Street. It was very busy. There was a big crowd waiting there. Then we saw soldiers march past us in red uniforms with black busbies on their heads.

After this, we went into the department store and bought some toys for my sand pit. Then, we had some lunch in the restaurant. It was pizza with a big plate of chips. They brought it to our table and it was delicious.

When I went home, it was so sunny that my mum said she would fill up the paddling pool. I had fun splashing around in it.

Then I had my dinner and went to bed. I enjoyed my day, because I had so much fun.

My Trip to the Bird Park

I went to the Bird Park on Tuesday afternoon with my friend. When we got out of the car, it started to rain heavily, so my friend's mum had to buy us raincoats from the shop.

First, we went into the Sea Life centre. We saw lots of different types of tropical fish, some big, grey sharks, and two crocodiles, hiding in the vegetation of their enclosure. The little sea horses were also very sweet.

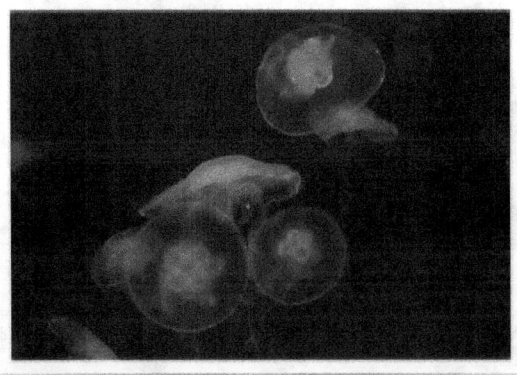

After this, we walked round the park in the pouring rain and we were jumping over the puddles. We saw lots of colourful birds. <u>My favourite one was the toucan.</u> He has a long, curved and brightly coloured beak to help him eat fruit. There were lots of colourful parrots and macaws. They wanted to eat my packet of bird seed, though they were not meant to have it. <u>I thought the ostrich was quite proud because he kept strutting backwards and forwards.</u>

At the end of my visit, I went to the shop and bought a balloon in the shape of a toucan. Then, we went home for tea and I went to bed.

To Help You

Draw a picture

In the .... I went to ....
with .... We went in ....
It was ....

When we had parked the car, we walked ......
.... There was ....
....

We saw ....

After this, we went ....
....
....
....

Draw a picture

In the summer holiday I went to ....
.... with ....
It was ....
We drove there in ....

When we got there we ....
.... I ....
.... and ....
I also enjoyed ....

What I enjoyed most was ....
....
.... because ....
....

"Wherever I look there is something to read or write," says Isabella.

Come on friends, read this. It is an invitation to my party.

Fill in the missing information.

Come to my PIRATE PARTY

On ....
At ....
Times ....

Come in your costume.
RSVP

Come to my PRINCESS PARTY

On ....
At ....
Times ....

Come in your costume.
RSVP

After the party, we have to send some thank you notes for our presents.

Dear Grandad,

Thank you for the big pack of Lego you bought me. I like it very much. I can use it with my other Lego sets to build a giant town. I am enjoying playing with it.

        Love,

        Skye

Dear ....,

Thank you for my pencil case. It is just what I wanted for school. I have put my pencils and pens in it for Monday. See you soon.

        Love,

        ....

Dear ....,

Thank you for the new t-shirt you bought me. It suits me very well and I am wearing it a lot.

Love,

....

Dear ....,

Thank you for ....
....
....
....
....
....

Love,

....

Hooray! It is half term. Let us help mum make our dinner. She will need:

- 400 g of spaghetti
- 1 kg of ripe tomatoes
- 1 clove of garlic
- 1 onion
- 1 carrot
- 1 slice of celery
- Some basil leaves
- Oil
- Grated parmesan cheese

1. **Wash** tomatoes
2. **Chop** them
3. **Put** the vegetables in a pan with the garlic and some salt and pepper
4. **Boil** gently for one hour
5. **Cook** pasta for eight minutes
6. **Drain** it and put it on a plate
7. **Pour** the sauce over
8. **Sprinkle** with cheese

Instructions start with commands (imperative verbs).

...and let us help mum make some sweets for our friends. Mum needs:

- 75g soft cheese
- 1 tablespoon of milk
- 100g of icing sugar
- 100g of chocolate powder
- chocolate sprinkles

1. **Wash** your hands.
2. **Mix** the milk and cheese
3. **Stir** in the icing sugar and the chocolate powder.
4. **Form** into balls with your hands.
5. **Roll** them in chocolate sprinkles.
6. **Leave** in fridge to set.

We need to find the address in my address book:

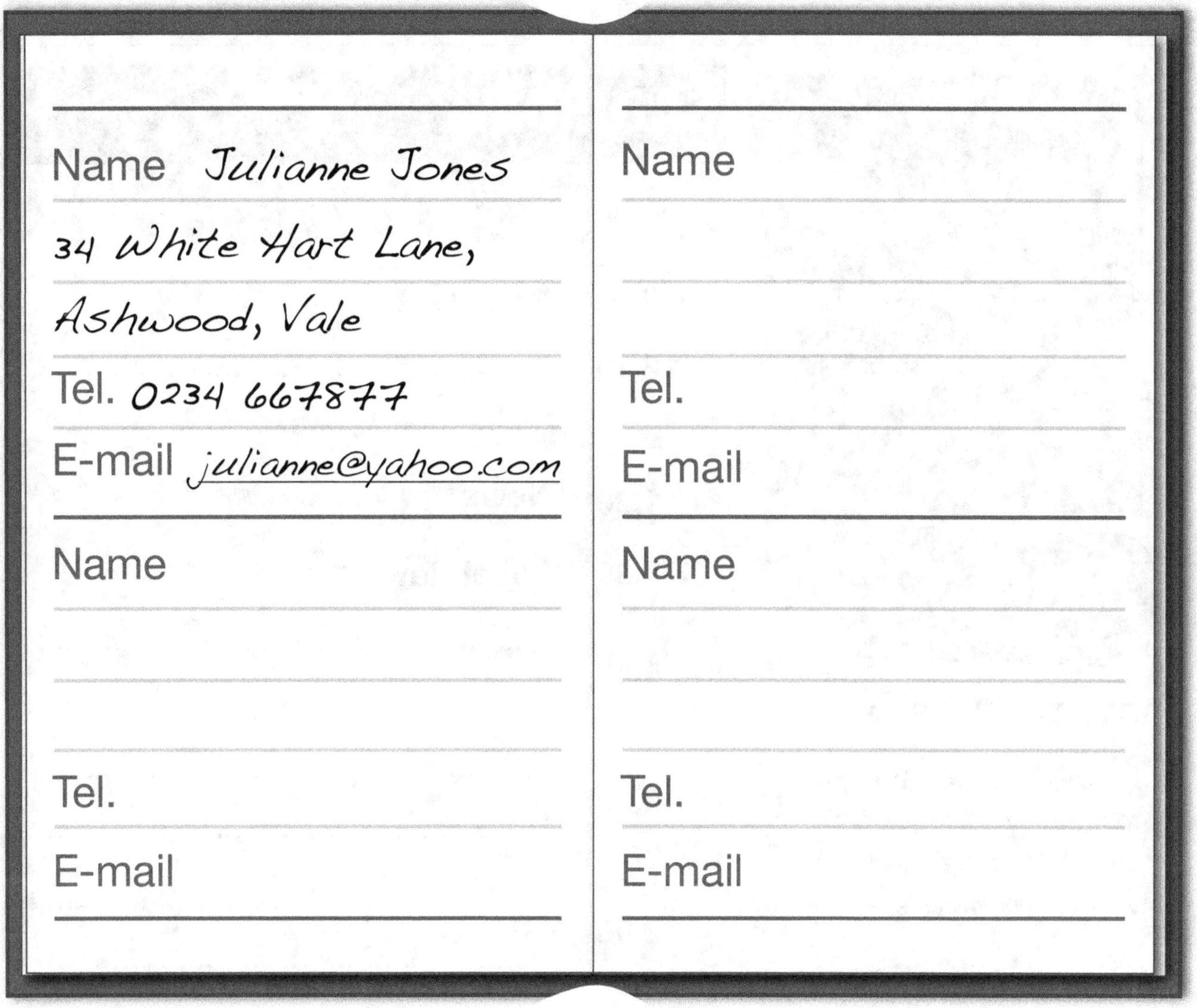

Name *Julianne Jones*

34 White Hart Lane,
Ashwood, Vale

Tel. *0234 667877*

E-mail *julianne@yahoo.com*

Name

Tel.

E-mail

Name

Tel.

E-mail

Name

Tel.

E-mail

We think we will watch TV today. Can we read what is on? Fill in this list of programmes.

★ STAR'S CHOICE

DOG TALENT SHOW   **ITV**

Watch ten talented dogs go head to head in this fun, new show. Judge their different tricks and vote for your favourite.

MUST SEE

My favourite show is
....
....
because ....
....
....
....

SATURDAY
BBC1

6.00	Breakfast
12.15	....
	....
1.00	News
1.30	Local News
1.45	....
	....
2.15	....
	....
3.00	....
	....
3.30	....
	....
4.00	....
	....
5.00	....
	....
5.30	....
	....
6.00	News
7.00	The Daily Show

Let us go out somewhere. First, we must read the poster.

The **AMAZING** ice skating rink is coming to ....

On ....

At ....

Open daily from ....

PRICE:

Children .... Adult ....

Phone .... for ticket information.

Write some posters.

SANTA'S <u>WINTER WONDERLAND</u> EXPERIENCE

at .... Park

Open on ....

Until ....

Times ....

Walk along our snowy winter wonderland trail to see Santa's reindeer. Visit the <u>amazing grotto</u>. Kids get a present.

KIDS FUN DAY

at .... on ....

times ....

A day of fun:
- ★ Fabulous **face painting** for kids of all ages
- ★ **Fun fair**
- ★ Entertainment all day - **clowns**, **jugglers**
- ★ **Bouncy Castle**

Puppy OBEDIENCE Classes

At ....

On ....

Times ....

Is your puppy naughty? Bring it along to obedience classes. **Your puppy will never be naughty again**. It will learn to sit, to stay, to take a treat without grabbing, and not to jump up at people. You and your puppy will also make lots of friends.

at .... on ....

times ....

Have fun at Rico's Circus. Be amazed by the jugglers and acrobats as they perform their tricks.

Posters can be persuasive and full of opinions. Can you spot any?

Let us make a felt puppet.

1. Cut two identical bear shapes out of felt.
2. Get an adult to help you glue or sew round the shapes.
3. Turn it right side out.
4. Stick on two eyes and a mouth.

Let us make a picture.

1. Draw an owl.
2. Spread glue on the picture.
3. Press on pieces of pasta, lentils and rice.
4. Leave to dry.

Let us make a flower.

1. Cut out two flower shapes.
2. Stick one each side of a straw.
3. Draw a leaf, cut it out and stick it on the straw.

Let us go the the library. Let us read a non-fiction book.

Title	What is this book about?
The Big Book of Elephants	Facts and information about the lives of elephants in their natural habitat.

Let's go for a walk round Heathervale Park but first, we must read the map.

> To get to the park:
>
> 1. From the motorway bridge turn left.
> 2. Go to the end of the road.
> 3. Turn right and continue straight on until you reach the car park.
> 4. The park entrance is in front of you.

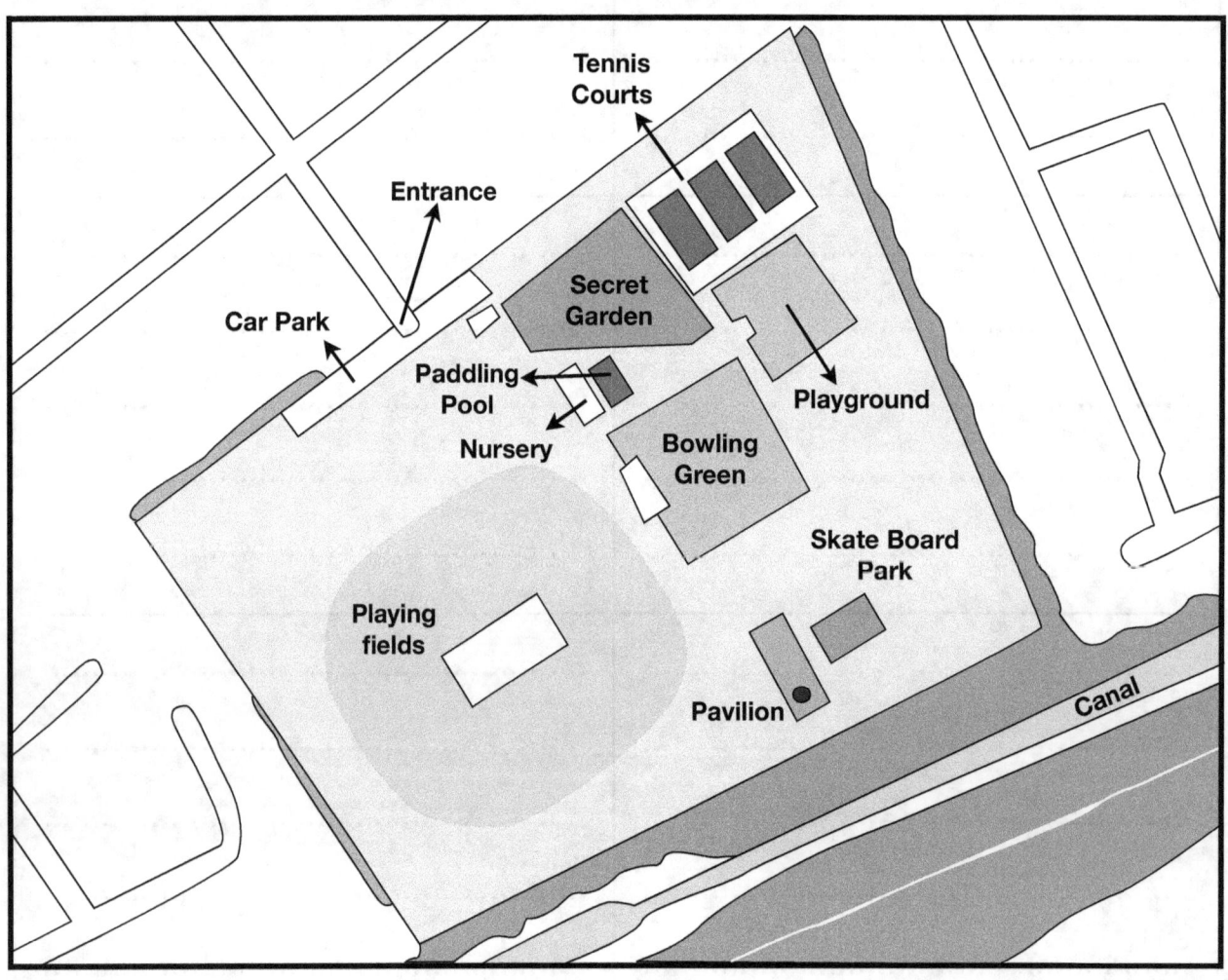

We are on holiday. We must send greetings to our friends.

Dear ....

I am having a great time in Turkey. The flight was good. The weather is hot and sunny. I have visited the Topaki Palace and have been for a boat trip on the river.

　　　　Love ,

　　　..........................

Dear ....

We our staying in our caravan. It is in the New Forest so I have seen loads of New Forest Ponies.

　　　　Love ,

　　　..........................

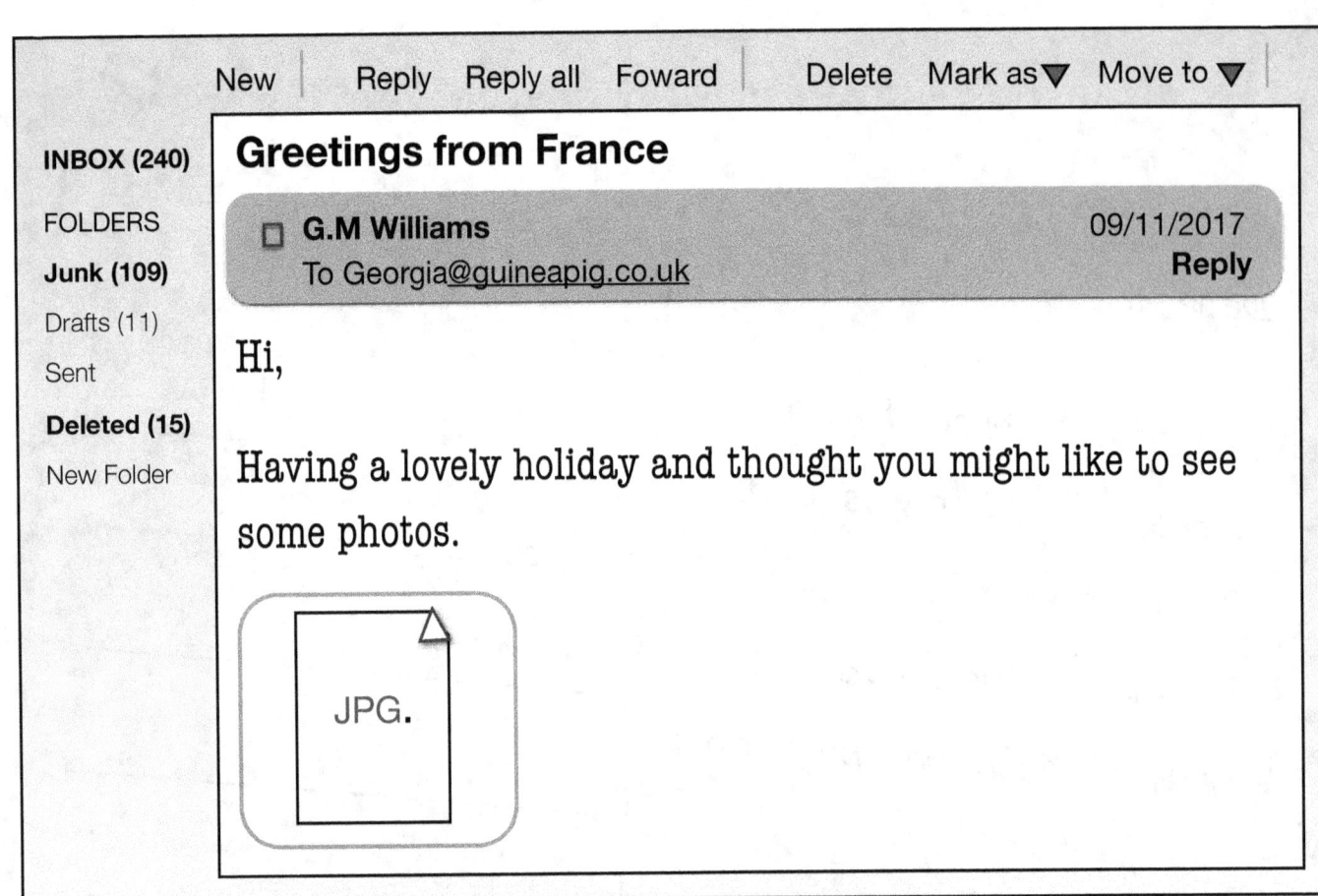

It is nearly Christmas. I need a wish list.

My Christmas Wish List

....

.... teddy bear

....

....

Christmas presents to buy

MUM	DAD	....	....
....	....	....	....
....	....	....	....
....	....	....	....

Letter to Santa to be put in chimney at Grotto.

Do not fuss too much over correct spelling, but encourage your child to get their ideas down.

★ Encourage your child to make their own dictionary. Cut up an exercise book, so there is one page for each letter.

★ Be prepared to give your child help with writing the words down.

★ If your child prefers to get their own ideas down, encourage them to sound out words using phonic blends (i.e. J a ck and the B ea n st alk). They will get more accurate spelling this way.

★ If your child is a fluent reader, use a children's dictionary to look up words they do not know.

★ Make sure your child remembers to use punctuation, like capital letters, full stops and question marks.

Get over this message early on.

Stories and books are **GREAT**...

AMAZING!

It is **FUN** to read.

Later on so many children stop reading and prefer computer games or watching TV. Here are some ways we can help:

- Parents: sit with your child and read the pages from your child's school reading book, working out new words using phonics.

- Encourage children to choose books from the library or book club to read or to have read aloud.

Some children need to be encouraged. We can help them build up confidence in reading and writing skills.

- Parents: read bedtime stories with your child.

- Get your child to recount stories they have heard on TV, DVD, films and at story time.

Parents: when you read a story, talk about it with your child. Ask your child, if they know:

- Who is in it?
- Where they are?
- What is happening?
- What they think will happen next?
- How they expect the story to end?
- What they liked best or why it happened?

Encourage you child not to give you one-word answers, but to use lots of detail when they talk about what is happening in the story.

Encourage them:

- To explain clearly why they think something is happening in a story.

- To give reasons as to what they think it means for the characters.

IMPORTANT

Yes even at this stage!

Encourage your child to think beneath the surface, to form his or her own opinions.

Your child will read every day:

- in shops, along streets
- on posters and notices
- on T.V., on invitations
- on instructions, ingredients

    and so on....

When you are out and about, ask your child questions. Can you read the sign? What does it mean?

www.ingramcontent.com/pod-product-compliance
Lightning Source LLC
Chambersburg PA
CBHW050715090526
44587CB00019B/3392